Handel's Bestiary

Donna Leon

Handel's Bestiary

In Search of Animals in Handel's Operas

Illustrated by
Michael Sowa

Music by George Frideric Handel
with

Alan Curtis
conducting Il Complesso Barocco

Atlantic Monthly Press

New York

Published simultaneously in Canada
Printed in the United States of America

FIRST EDITION

ISBN-13: 978-0-8021-1996-4

Atlantic Monthly Press
an imprint of Grove/Atlantic, Inc.
841 Broadway
New York, NY 10003

Distributed by Publishers Group West
www.groveatlantic.com

11 12 13 14 15   10 9 8 7 6 5 4 3 2 1

Contents

Foreword

Subtract the motor. Cancel it from your consciousness: switch it off, as it were. Then take a new look at the world, or – better said – take a look at the way the world was before so much of it was changed by the arrival of the motor and all it brought along with it. Suddenly the order of importance given to certain things will change. Who needs oil? Where can I find a good riding horse?

One of the first recalibrations that the absence of the motor demands is a re-shifting of the order of creation that will allow animals to return to their former importance. The muscle power of man, made pretty much redundant by the arrival of the machine, will still be inferior to that of an ox, and his ability to move quickly from place to place will again depend upon the speed of the horse. Not only did animals supply muscle power, but their ownership and husbandry was one of the principal bases of wealth, and thus power, in the pre-industrial world.

Returning to former times will also cause us to lose access to those sources that today provide us with information about the world we live in – the printed book, films, television, the internet – and leave us once again dependent upon the means which informed past ages of the world around them: oral tradition, legend, and manuscript. The importance of the role played by animals in these sources cannot be overstated.

Man lived with animals and around animals, and thus their abilities and habits were the stuff of common knowledge and of common reference. Folk tales were filled with their antics, their cunning, and their sense of independence, and much moral instruction was based upon their observed – or imputed – behavior. Leftovers of this come down in the English-speaking world in expressions like "Cunning as a fox," "Brave as a lion," "Dirty as a pig," "Wily as a serpent."

The attributes which common wisdom linked to various animals were often based upon direct observation: foxes *are* cunning, and lions *are* brave, and a mother tiger *will* defend her young at any cost. But much was based on other sources, among which – at least in Europe – was the Bible, which probably explains the bad reputation of the snake, who is really quite a helpful chap, gobbling up insects and vermin. Much received wisdom about animals also filtered down from the *Natural History* of Pliny the Elder and the *Etymologies* of Isidore of Seville, as well as from that great historian, Herodotus.

Information – well, what passed for information – about animals also had a way of slipping in from other cultures and from sketches and verbal accounts brought back from travelers in foreign lands. Thus the pictorial representation of animals which had been described but never seen displayed a certain inventiveness. A manuscript from Northern France (ca. 1300) pictures what is meant to be an elephant but which actually looks like a friendly dog with pig tusks, from between which emerges something that looks like a cross between a walrus horn and a vacuum cleaner. In one later bestiary, a painting of what is often said to be a sloth, might just as easily be a curly-haired mouse with inordinately large feet. These early manuscripts also contain an inventive menagerie of dragons and demons, sirens and centaurs, as well as griffons and unicorns. There are also ox-headed Saint Lukes and sheep-headed pastors.

Strangely enough, only a century later artists other than the ones who illustrated the Bestiaries were even then painting, sketching, and drawing perfect pictures of animals and birds, accurate to the most minute detail. The Biblioteca Civica of Bergamo possesses the notebook of Giovannino de Grassi with drawings of birds and animals so real that they seem only perched on the page, ready to fly off into reality. Or consider for a moment all of those perfectly rendered dogs sitting under the tables where Christ is eating the last supper or noblemen are feasting. But the business of the Bestiary was to teach, not to render an accurate pictorial record, and the craftsmen who illustrated them were a world away in talent from the artists who were in the process of opening Europe's eyes.

Man is an imaginative creature who delights in making connections between the real world and a higher world. Thus the perceived virtues and vices of animals are often made to resonate in the human sphere to serve as examples from which moral lessons can be drawn to the edification and improvement of fallen mankind. Mickey Mouse did not conquer the world because he is a fool; Goofy's name is not an accident.

Though this tradition is Medieval and pre-Medieval, certainly these habits of thought and association filtered down into the Eighteenth Century to become part and parcel of the mental baggage of writers, poets, and – of concern here – opera librettists. The qualities attributed to animals served, and still serve, as a sort of moral shorthand, and so reference to a lion in an aria would summon with it the courage that is traditionally attributed to that animal, the noblest of them all. To fill an aria about a snake with sibilant words and then to set it to a sinuous rhythm would enforce the association with the chief enemy of mankind.

Handel's operas and oratorios are filled with arias that make reference to animals: sometimes they are invoked as templates of virtuous behavior, while occasionally they serve a more malign purpose, like the frogs who invade the land of the Egyptians, "even in the king's chambers." Occasionally – as with the mother tiger who pops into the third act of *Alcina* – their arrival is conventional and formulaic, as if Handel had kept this wonderful aria in his back pocket for some time, and this was as good a place as any to use it. Quite the contrary seems the case of the silver dove in *Theodora,* who sings longingly of the freedom of the bird to fly to the eternal peace of Heaven, a perfect symbol of Theodora's own spiritual desire.

The thought of this collection of arias had been percolating in my mind for some time, as it had in that of like-minded Handel enthusiast, Alan Curtis. Then when I introduced him to the artist Michael Sowa, we both decided he would be the ideal person to help us realize this project visually. I recalled that while at university I had read widely in the Medieval bestiaries as well as in the texts of the early natural historians and remained, thirty years on, utterly charmed by the stories they had to tell. So we decided to combine our efforts in what we hope will be an adequate tribute to this most genial and inventive of composers, to the early writers who first set down these legends, and to the animals that served as the focus of Handel's genius.

LION

LION

Qual leon che fere irato
From: ARIANNA IN CRETA
Act 2, scene 6

Qual leon che fere irato,
se sua prole altri involò:
tale anch'io di sdegno armato
nella pugna ferirò.

Ma se avvien che l'idol mio
renda pago il mio desio,
pace e calma sol avrò.

Like an enraged lion
Whose young have been stolen,
So will I, armed with anger,
Strike in battle.

But should my love
Give me my desires,
Then I will have only peace and tranquility.

The lion is the animal which appears most frequently in the Bestiaries, where his picture and story take pride of place by appearing first. This imitates his position in the world of animals, where he is king of the beasts, the first among non-equals. Genesis is often interpreted to contain the prophecy that the lion of Judah will produce the ruler for whom the world waits: thus, if Christ is to become the King of Heaven, his animal representative must surely serve that position among the animals of the earth. One has but to take a careful look at other lions that serve as visual symbols, from the three lions *passant guardant* on the flag of the Plantagenets (put there by Richard the – yes – Lionhearted) and now the official arms of England, to the lion *rampant* used to sell a French automobile, to realize how universally the lion is associated with majesty and power.

This reputation has a long history, though had the Greek historian Herodotus had the facts right, the race of lions would have been of short duration. Herodotus believed that the female lion gives birth only once in her life because her unborn cub, as soon as he begins to stir inside her womb, also begins to scratch at it with his claws, rather in the fashion of a house cat with a sofa. Thus, when he is finally born, he has effectively destroyed her womb, which is expelled with him. Herodotus obviously never troubled himself with the mathematical consequences, which would surely lead to the extinction of the lion.

Pliny the Elder was also concerned with the birth habits of the lion and postulated that she gives birth, the first time, to five cubs. Each subsequent year she bears one less, until she becomes barren after the fifth year, though not before producing fifteen cubs. These cubs are born dead but are brought into life, after three days, either by the licking or the roaring of their father, an event in which Christian apologists saw the parallel with the three-day death of Christ which preceded the Resurrection.

Social historians might well be moved to seek the origin of bulimia in the lion for, according to Pliny the Elder, when he ate too much, he reached down into his throat and clawed the meat out of his stomach. Should the lion be put off his food in response to this, he has but to taste the blood of a monkey for his appetite to be restored.

Lions were believed to sleep with their eyes open and were known to obliterate their tracks by brushing them away with their tails. They are afraid of the sound of wheels and terrified of fire. Though thought to be fierce and merciless, the lion is actually an example of kindness, for he will never harm anyone who prostrates himself on the ground before him. Given political changes taking place during the Middle Ages, this shift in the behavior which the Bestiaries attributed to the lion might well reflect a growing belief that the just monarch is also the merciful monarch.

Certainly this is evident in the airbrushing done to the reputation of Richard the Lionhearted, said to have earned the nickname either by the savagery of his treatment of Sicilians or by having eaten the heart of a lion he killed with his bare hands. By the thirteenth century, however, a historian was hastening to add that Richard, like the lion, "put on reason and kindness." About the same time, an ecclesiastical historian remarks that "The noble lion's wrath can spare the vanquished/ Do likewise all who govern on this earth."

Handel's aria, "Qual leon," was written for Margherita Durastanti, Handel's longest-serving singer, and gives her the chance to sing full force of revenge and punishment. She had created Agrippina for him in Venice a quarter of a century earlier and, with the passing of time, had become famous for trouser roles. In this aria, the horns are included for their power and for the sheer volume of sound they provide to accompany great bravura singing, to make no mention of their association with hunting. They are present in the opening section of the aria, disappear in the middle section, which speaks of peace and calm, only to return in full force in the da capo, along with pairs of oboes and bassoons. Durastanti was no longer a spring chicken (an animal about which Handel wrote no aria) but amazing leaps of an octave or more show that her voice had lost none of its legendary agility.

21

SNAKE

SNAKE

L'angue o eso mai riposa
From: GIULIO CESARE IN EGITTO
Act 2, scene 6

24

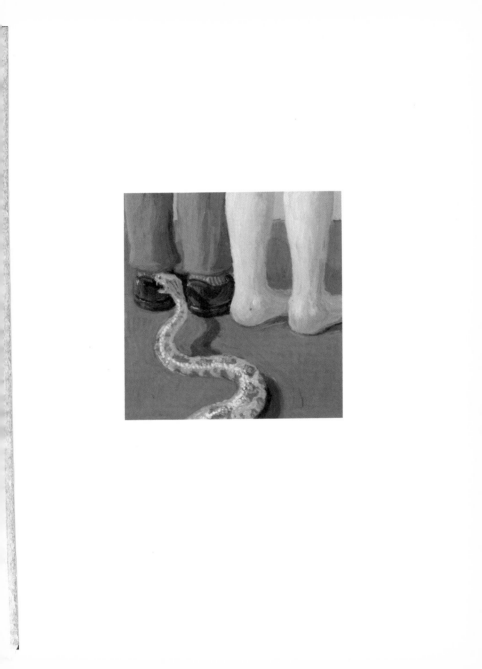

Figlio non è, chi vendicar non cura
del genitor lo scempio.
Su, dunque, alla vendetta
ti prepara, alma forte,
e, prima di morir, altrui da' morte!

L'angue o eso mai riposa,
se il veleno pria non spande
dentro il sangue all'o ensor.
Così l'alma mia non osa
di mostrarsi altera e grande,
se non svelle l'empio cor.

He is no son who does not
Seek to revenge his father's murder.
Come then, my strong spirit,
Prepare for vengeance
And before death, kill the enemy.

The angry snake never rests,
Until he has sunk his poison
Into the blood of his enemy.

Thus my angered spirit can never
Call itself mighty or grand
Until it has destroyed that evil heart.

We don't need much more than Genesis 3 to give us an idea of the way Western culture is going to regard the snake, do we? Disguised as a serpent, Satan deceives Eve into believing that to eat the apple will make her and Adam godlike, and then he effectively disappears from the story. But he leaves behind him that faint whiff of sulfur commonly believed to remain after visits by all things demonic. The snake corrupts man and his life, leads to the Fall from Grace, and thus makes necessary the Redemption.

Those of us who have grow up with this automatic association between snake and sin, heirs as well to the atavistic fear of snakes - the one that allowed Emily Dickinson to say that the sudden sight of a snake leaves us feeling "zero at the bone" - will perhaps be surprised to learn that previous cultures revered and venerated them. The Romans, who were to co-opt Christianity, certainly had a positive view of snakes. They were associated with fertility and healing (look at the caduceus, with its twining snakes) and often represented the spirits of the dead, though in a benign fashion.

But once he gave that apple to Eve, it was history for the serpent. The writers of the medieval bestiaries did not bother much to distinguish between the snake and the dragon and, for that matter, between the snake and many other creepy-crawlies. There was an enormous sub-set of reptiles, varying in size and deadliness, some no longer than the breadth of two fingers, while others, like the dragon, were big enough to strangle an elephant. This, as it turns out, was not a wise thing for a dragon to do, for as soon as he winds himself about the elephant and crushes him, "his victory He joyes not long; for his huge Enemy Falling down dead, doth with his weighty Fall Crush him to death, that caus'd his death withall."

Also listed in the family of the snake were a host of other creatures of greater or lesser unpleasantness. There was the Basilisk, whose glance could kill a man; the viper, vicious even before birth, which they achieved by gnawing through the sides of their mother, to "burst out to her destruction." There is also the Hydra, who covers himself in mud and jumps into the mouths of sleeping crocodiles, slides down into their bellies and comes out the other end; and the Boa, which clings to the udders of buffaloes and milks them dry. For poison it is hard to beat the Salamander: it has but to twine about the trunk of a fruit tree to render its crop deadly, to fall into a well to kill all who drink the water. The salamander cannot burn, even if hurled into a fire. Interestingly enough, when asbestos was discovered, it was believed to be the wool of this creature (a woolly reptile?).

As if these facts were not enough, there remained three unusual things that it was necessary to know about snakes.

1. When they are old and going blind (assuming that they had not availed themselves of the well-known remedy for snake-blindness and eaten some fennel), they crawl away somewhere and fast for at least forty days, which shrinks them and loosens their skins. Then they crawl through a narrow crack in the rocks, which scrapes off the old skin and rejuvenates them.

2. Before drinking water from a river, a snake will spit all of its poison in a hole.

3. A snake will never attack a naked man, only one wearing clothing. Though this was certainly an advantage for Adam, it is perhaps not good news for hikers.

To avoid risk, hikers might be advised to employ the tactic of the tortoise, which protects itself by eating fresh marjoram (some manuscripts advise oregano) when it sees a venomous creature sneaking up on it. Or, if the hiker has been fasting for some time, he might persuade the serpent to drink his spittle, which will cause its death.

The snake insinuates itself into Handel's Giulio Cesare when Sesto, son of the murdered Pompey, vows to take vengeance against Tolomeo, his father's killer. He pumps up his spirit with a short recitative and then proclaims that, like an angered snake that never rests until it has "spilled its poison in his enemy's blood," he too will have vengeance. The aria twines and retwines around itself as Sesto – a Roman and thus an admirer of snakes – gives himself up fully to his desire for revenge. Not only is the music serpentine: sibilants seep from every line of the text as the young Sesto vows to sink his poison into the blood of his enemy.

NIGHTINGALE

NIGHTINGALE

Nasconde l'usignol' in alti rami il nido
From: DEIDAMIA
Act 1, scene 5

Da questi scaltri ospiti greci è d'uopo
lunge tener, quanto possibil fia,
il travestito Achille,
l'amata anima mia.
In dolce corrisposto a etto ascoso
chi è di me più felice?
Soccorri i tuoi seguaci, Amor pietoso!

Nasconde l'usignol'
in alti rami il nido
al serpe e al cacciator,
ma il volo spesso e fido
dove lo porta amor
che il può tradir non sa.

Lontana sì, ma in pene,
quest'alma dal suo bene
più l'arte ingannerà.

From these quick-sighted, crafty Grecian guests,
Disguised Achilles, my soul's beloved,
Must strive to keep at distance all he can.
O who can ever be so blessed as I,
In a concealed, most sweet, and mutual love?
Look down, o deity of pleasing pains!
Assist thy votaries, thou gentle god!

From serpent and fowler's snare,
On branches trembling high in air.
The nightingale her nest conceals;
But yet she has not learned to know
That love, which brings her to and fro,
With ease the hiding place reveals.

What though in pain I pass the day,
From my beloved far away,
If by that means I cheat the eyes
Of dangerous and artful spies.

The bestiaries teem with fluttering birds, all manner of them, so many that "it is not possible to learn every one." Some sing beautifully, some try to imitate the voices of men, while some can do no more than make raucous noises. Their names are sometimes onomatopoeic - just think of the gru (crane) or the cuckoo - and their appearance varies wildly – think of the difference between the sparrow and the ostrich. In general, they are called aves (a-ves) because they often fly in wild, inventive patterns and are not constrained to follow the paths (vias) built by man.

This freedom from constraint has long fascinated humans, whom the birds left behind to tread the earth: their freedom to travel a wider world was perhaps instrumental in helping to transform them into easily recognizable symbols of liberty and freedom. Because they have direct contact with the heavens, and thus greater proximity to the gods, birds were perceived by both the Greeks and Romans as emissaries from the Divine: did not Mercury, the messenger of the gods, have wings on his heels? The patterns of their flight served to reveal the will of the gods, and the future was often read in a close examination of their entrails.

The Romans judged most important the eagle, the pugnacious bird which best symbolized the power and glory of their empire, and whose image was borne on the standards of their legions. Subsequent real and wannabe empires adopted the image of the eagle, often giving it two heads, the better to keep an eye (er, eyes) on things. Eagles perch all over the standards of empire: Byzantium, Napoleon's France, the Holy Roman Empire, Austria, Russia, and try to give a touch of majesty to some modern computer games that have to do with conquest.

Pliny the Elder tells us that the eagle was responsible for the death of Aeschylus, the Greek dramatist, who was killed by a turtle that was dropped on his head by a passing eagle. Often, the ancients came up with fantastical explanation for observed phenomena. The process of moulting, for example, was believed to occur when the aged eagle, to renew his vigor and extend his life, flew close enough to the sun to singe away his feathers, after which he plunged into a fountain three times, to emerge "renewed with a great vigor of plumage."

More helpful, perhaps, but no less pugnacious are the geese of Rome, whose cackles woke the ex-consul Manlius in 390 B. C. just in time to lead his troops to defend the Capitoline from the invading Gauls.

Less aggressive, but no less military, are the cranes, who often have to fly their light bodies into the face of strong winds. To do so safely, they tank up on sand and small stones before take-off, thus giving themselves the ballast necessary to stabilize their flight. A strong-voiced navigator always flies at the tip of their formation; should any of the birds in the squadron grow tired, others will approach them and provide support until they are rested enough to resume flight on their own. When the birds alight in the evening, guards are posted to patrol the area around their sleeping flock-mates. Each guard carries a stone in one claw so that, should he fall asleep during the watch, the sound of the falling stone will wake him.

Some birds have the gift of speech. The teachers of parrots – in these effete, politically correct times in which we live – might well serve as clandestine models for all teachers. Should some parrots prove recalcitrant at learning to speak, the Bestiaries advise that they be encouraged with a few solid whacks with an iron rod. Might this explain the origin of the conductor's baton?

Sirens were, for many of the Bestiaries, another kind of bird, a half-human bird, though at times this proportion shrank to a third, for the Siren was sometimes part fish as well as part bird. What was never in question, however, was their relentless desire to lure sailors – unable to resist the beauty of their song - to their doom. Paracelsus opines that sirens have no souls, but if they marry a man, "now they have the soul." Useful to know.

Moral lessons were never far to seek in the pages of the Bestiaries. The peacock, for all the glory of his tail, was forever kept from vanity by the sight of his feet, which were so ugly, Bartolomeus Anglicus tells us, as to cause him to lower his tail to hide them. Storks, which will moult all of their feathers to create the nests for their chicks, are then in turn nursed through their featherless times by those same chicks. Similarly, the hoopoe restore their elderly parents by preening their feathers for them to keep them warm and licking their eyes so that they can see, thus setting another example of proper parental-filial comportment.

The nightingale, another dedicated parent, sits all night upon her eggs, keeping them safe from enemies, and filling the dark with her glorious song. There is great rivalry between nightingales to see who can sing most beautifully, so great that the bird judged to be the loser will often die of shame.

One has but to think of the famous story told of the battle that erupted on stage between Francesca Cuzzoni and Faustina Bordoni (later Hasse), Handel's greatest prima donnas, to see how very competitive songbirds could be. Appearing together in Bononcini's Astianatte, neither of these nightingales gave a thought to dying of shame: instead, they came to blows. In itself, this sort of violent rivalry was not unique: what turned it into a scandal was the presence of the Princess of Wales among the public. It is also reported that a male member of the audience, hearing Cuzzoni sing on some other occasion, cried out, "Damn her. She has a nest of nightingales in her belly."

It is worth noting that most of the arias about animals that Handel wrote for the soprano voice refer to birds and are written in A major. Further, the break-off point in those arias – in fact, for almost all of Handel's soprano arias - is high a: he seldom took them above that note. Although Handel's audiences would have considered both Faustina and Cuzzoni to be sopranos, the stricter distinctions drawn between voice types in today's opera world would describe Faustina as a high mezzo.

In the aria from his last opera, Deidamia, Handel provides his eponymous (how I have always longed to use that word) heroine with a musical depiction of birdsong filled with short, chirping motives, sometimes repeated, sometimes not. The motive in the violins of two notes a mere half step apart, separated by a rest, then repeated, effectively imitates the call of the nightingale.

He does not transfer this directly to the voice but gives her repeated staccato notes, gradually increasing in speed but not related to words in the text, and thus all the more likely to sound like the chirping of a bird. The aria is sung by Deidamia, who wants NOT to be like a nightingale, who hides her young in a nest high (sung on a high a) in a tree and thus, flying back and forth to the nest, often leads the hunters right to them. In order to protect her lover Achille from the Greeks who are searching (hunting?) for him, she determines to remain far from him. But still, in an ascending flight of nearly two octaves, she gives aural evidence of her longing to fly to her beloved, and to hell with the risk.

BEE

BEE

Vedi l'ape
From: BERENICE, REGINA D'EGITTO
Act 1, scene 3

Vedi l'ape ch'ingegnosa
su quei fior vola e si posa
dove più trova d'umor.

Né s'arresta, ancorché bello
sembri a lei di questo e quello
solo e semplice il color.

Observe the clever bee,
Who flies from flower to flower,
Settling where it finds most nectar.

It does not stop to observe
Each flower it sees
Simply because it is beautiful.

W ell, we can't have female power, can we? And a Queen? With power? In the Middle Ages? Are you off your head? Thus the King Bee. Yes, it does sound strange, doesn't it: a King Bee? But what better evidence of the fact that the Bestiary reflected, not only the natural history of the Middle Ages, but the social, political, and moral ideas of an era when female power could be viewed only with suspicion: after all, one must never forget where Eve led us all. Before that, however, in the less-restrictive pagan world, Pliny the Elder wrote with great admiration of the Queen Bee and acknowledged that the bee population showed a "remarkable obedience to her."

To the medieval world, bees were not only wonderful birds; they were also the smallest sort of birds. They originated in the decomposing bodies of oxen, sometimes those of calves. Their name originates from their being born without feet (pes) and so they are a-pes. Luckily, their feet arrive later, along with the wings.

Their virtuous nature is reflected in the upright, orderly nature of the houses they construct for themselves and in their instinctive preference for hard work to sex. In fact, they so much prefer work that they reproduce spontaneously: one has only to beat the body of dead ox, and what comes forth are bees. Should you be curious: wasps emerge from asses and hornets from horses, all of them, it seems, equally uninterested in sex.

Bees were believed to be unique in the animal world in that they raise their children in common and in the fact that, should they be caught out overnight, they lie on their backs to protect their wings from the dew and rain, the better to rise up with the sun the next morning and get back to work directly.

The natural order of society is reflected in bees, as well, for they have that king, have armies, and go forth to battle. So devoted to the perpetuation of their society are they that they are strangers to theft and know only, as mentioned previously, work. Peaceful creatures, should it happen that they are moved to use their sting, regret forces them to lie themselves down to die in the wound they created. Further, should they do something which angers the king or breaks one of the bee-laws, they gladly sting themselves and happily die, a custom thought to be common to the Persian people, as well.

The king to whom they are so eagerly obedient is one whom they have chosen themselves and to whom they gladly offer their loyalty and their love. That this particular bee must be king is perhaps already evident, for he stands forth "by virtue of the size and appearance of his body." He is also "most worthy and noble in highness and fairness and most clear in mildness, for this is the chief virtue in a king." Though his greater size thus endows him with a larger sting, he refrains from using it, thus following the natural law which dictates that those endowed of greater power must be lenient in its use.

The bee is gracious and generous to mankind because he provides honey for him, and honey, we are repeatedly told by ancient writers, is a wondrous substance, both sweet and nourishing, and perhaps because of that, a perfect symbol for human richness and prosperity. Not only does honey provide sweetness and food; honey can, as well, soothe the inflamed throat, and the ground-up bodies of burnt bees, when compounded with the excrement of shrew mice, can stimulate the growth of the beard.

The bees which illustrate the pages of various manuscripts display a difference in accuracy almost as wide as that which exists among the pictured elephants. Given the fact that bees are somewhat more plentiful in Europe than elephants, this is difficult to explain. The Municipal Library of Reims contains a 14th century manuscript with all-but perfect illustrations of bees, complete with their gossamer wings, while an almost contemporaneous manuscript from northern France contains drawings of winged creatures which look like flying baby squids in Halloween masks. A fourteenth century manuscript from Flanders shows three creatures that might well be flying fish, or perhaps birds with the banded pattern common to bees, though a hundred years earlier a British illustrator pictured bees quite accurately in a psalter. The hives, too, have in common only their conical shape: beyond that, the shape pictured could be anything from a helmet to a haystack.

The most famous musical bee is, of course, Rimsky-Korsakov's, which makes extensive and memorable use of the chromatic (half-step) scale to provide a buzzing effect. The aria which Handel wrote for his late opera, Berenice, is sung by the Roman Ambassador, Fabio, as he tries to persuade Alessandro, an Egyptian nobleman, to switch his love from one woman to another. The example to follow is, of course, the bee, the rhythm of whose restless flight from flower to flower is imitated by the non-stop mono-rhythmic triplet motion in the violins which leaps, as does the bee, from flower to flower. Since love must follow politics, Fabio believes that what he suggests to Alessandro must be as meaningless and effortless for him as is flight for the bee.

SILVER DOVE

SILVER DOVE

O that I on wings could rise
From: THEODORA
Act 2, scene 2

But why art thou disquieted, my soul? –
Hark! Heav'n invites thee in sweet rapt'rous strains
to join the ever-singing, ever-loving choir,
of saints and angels in the courts above.

O that I on wings could rise,
swiftly sailing through the skies,
as skims the silver dove!
That I might rest,
for ever blest,
with harmony and love.

The silver dove appears in Genesis 8:8 when it first flies off from Noah's hand but comes back to the ark when "she found no rest for the sole of her foot." After a week, when Noah set her free again, and she returned with an olive leaf in her beak, sure proof that the waters had finally begun to recede. After another week, Noah released her a third time, and "she returned not again unto him any more."

She does return in Matthew 3:16, when, at the baptism of Christ, the Spirit of God descends upon Him like a dove. Before that, however, the dove was sacred to Venus, the goddess of love, and was often pictured drawing her chariot through the heavens.

Religious writers seemed particularly drawn to the sweet-tempered bird, seeing it as the symbol of many forms of virtuous behavior. In the Thirteenth Century, Bartolomeus Anglicus saw it as the messenger of peace and meekness. Further, he tells his readers that, according to St. Ambrose, the dove served as a messenger and would gladly carry notes and letters back to the place where it was raised, for it "loveth kindly the place and the dwelling where it was first fed." Once it was generally known that the doves could be used for this purpose, its life was endangered, for it would be shot down by the arrows of those interested in reading the letters, this, alas, whether it was carrying them or not.

The writers of the bestiaries had surprisingly little to say about the dove, save that it is a simple bird and free of gall and looks lovingly on its mate. And so, instead of being the subject of an extended natural history, the silver dove became the first half of an extended list of similes, the other half of which was filled by the Preacher. The dove has a groan instead of a song, as does the Preacher, who groans over his own sins and those of others. Doves sit near streams so that, seeing the approach of a hawk, they can dive into the water to escape, while Preachers stay ever near the scriptures so that, upon the approach of the Devil, then can dive into the safety of the wisdom provided in its pages.

Want more? The dove nests in a hole in a rock, just as the Preachers nest in the wounds of Christ. Somewhere along the way, previously unmentioned, the dove has picked up the ability to recover its own sight; if the clear vision of truth has been lost to the Preacher by sin, he can recover it through the spirit of prophecy. And so the list continues.

We are brought up sharp by an account attributed to the poet Wordsworth. His wife, walking in the woods one day, overheard a passing farmer's wife say, "Oh, I do like doves." Mrs. Wordsworth was cheered by this love of nature manifest in a member of the lower orders until the woman added, "But, some like them in a pie; for my part, there's nothing like 'em stewed in onions."

The silver dove appears in Handel's oratorio, Theodora, as the symbol of her deepest wish. A Christian, Theodora has been condemned for refusing to worship the gods of Rome, but condemned not to the noble death of the martyr but to the far worse fate of becoming a common prostitute of the Roman soldiers who imprison her. Like all of us in times of trouble, she wishes she could fly away like a bird: the one that comes to her mind is the silver dove, perhaps because it is already so closely linked to virtuous behavior.

The aria opens with an exclamation on a high g in the violins – which is later to be repeated by Theodora with a passionate "Oh!" – followed by a sweeping rapid passage from the lowest to the highest register, taken up by the voice on the word "sailing" in the passage, "swiftly sailing through the skies, as skims the silver dove." The word "skims" is accompanied by a floating two-note repetition that suggests motion without effort, to imitate the motion of a bird as it skims though the skies on motionless wings. This aria, suitable for the yearning she feels for the joy she knows she will never achieve, is in the minor mode. The middle section, which speaks of being "Blest with harmony and love," moves appropriately to the relative major, but the da capo returns to the minor as Theodora moves closer to the fate she has decided to accept.

TIGER

TIGER

Sta nell'Ircana pietrosa tana
From: ALCINA
Act 3, scene 3

Sta nell'Ircana
pietrosa tana
tigre sdegnosa
e incerta pende,
se parte o attende
il cacciator.

Dal teso strale
guardar si vuole,
ma poi la prole
lascia in periglio.
Freme e l'assale
desio di sangue,
pietà del figlio;
poi vince amor.

In her rocky Hyrcanian lair,
The angry tigress waits, uncertain
Whether to flee or await the hunter.

She would protect herself from the arrow,
But that would leave her young in danger.
She trembles, filled with lust for blood
And fear for her babies: love proves stronger.

Literature is filled with tigers. There is William Blake's "Tyger, tyger burning bright, in the forests of the night," a troubling reminder that the same hand that created good also created evil, and then there is A. A. Milne's Tigger, beastliness replaced by whimsical charm. Bestiaries, too, are filled with tigers, strange beasts who sometimes wear their stripes but most often forget to do so. The artists who painted or drew tigers show little evidence of actually having seen one. The idea had certainly been disseminated that they were variegated in coloring, for many of them are speckled or dappled to a certain degree. But they tend to have spots, rather than stripes, and they are thin, with the body structure of hunting dogs.

The tiger bounds into the Western accounts in the first century, described by both Lucan and Pliny, and reported by Pomponius Mela as coming from Hyrcania, in Persia. Pliny first describes the theft of the cubs: mounted on a swift horse, a hunter will steal the cubs and begin his escape. As the pursuing mother grows dangerously near, the hunter lets fall one of the cubs, thus distracting the mother, who stops to save it. When the enraged mother again draws close to the hunter, he drops another cub, again to have her stop to rescue it. And in this way the hunter safely arrives at his ship with one cub still in his arms.

A thousand years later, the tiger remained, as did the hunter in search of her cubs. But the dropped cub had been replaced, over the centuries, by a glass ball which the hunter threw down in front of the mother when she drew dangerously close. Distracted by the motion, the tiger would pause to examine the ball and, seeing in it the image of a tiger, would assume it to be her cub and would pause to suckle it. Upon discovering the deception, the mother renewed her pursuit of the hunter, who would drop another ball. In this way, once again she was deprived of her cub, as the hunter, horse, and cub made it safely to a waiting ship.

The Medieval mind spent a great deal of time in search of Higher Meanings, usually religious and moral truths disguised by a layer of symbolism. The tiger, thus, can be seen as a symbol of maternal love, but she can just as easily be used as an example of human vanity, for what other motive could cause her to abandon her chase at the sight of herself in the mirror? Thus moralists could, and did, argue that she was waylaid by vanity and pride: it was always the female tiger who was deflected from her need to save her cubs by the sight of her own reflected image in the glass ball. What more shocking example of the dangers of female vanity?

The tiger, however, is also an image of courage and fidelity, and it is this tradition which imbues Ruggiero's final stand-and-deliver aria from the opera Alcina, "Sta nell'Ircana." The aria seems plunked down into the scene, almost by accident: this results from Handel's having cut the preceding recitative, which makes it clear that Ruggiero is assuring his true love, Bradamante, that he will defend her. Like the tiger, he is torn between conflicting desires, whether to flee or to stay and fight the hunter, and Ruggiero heroically decides to remain in place and defend what he loves. And love wins. He has waited almost the entire opera to declare himself both a hero and a warrior: after this showpiece aria, there can be no doubt that he is both of those things.

FROGS

FROGS

Their land brought forth frogs
From: ISRAEL IN EGYPT
Part II

Their land brought forth frogs
yea, even in their king's chambers.
He gave their cattle over to the pestilence;
blotches and blains broke forth on man and beast.

Why is it that one tends always to use the plural when speaking of or writing about frogs? Could it be that we never forget that childhood view of thousands and thousands of frog eggs floating on the surface of the pond at the end of the road or the countless hundreds of tiny tadpoles swimming in that same water some weeks later? Or the horrid fact that the Australian cane toad (really the Hawaiian cane toad, but imported to Australia in the 30's) lays 40,000 eggs at a go? Or perhaps it is the vision presented in Exodus 8 when "frogs came up, and covered the land of Egypt."

They also swarm around in the Tales of Aesop, the 6th century Greek collector of stories and allegories, filled with obvious moral messages: consider the consequences before you act, who puffs himself up too much will burst. Different cultures attribute different things to them. In Revelations, the Prophet sees "three unclean spirits like frogs come out of the mouth of the dragon," yet in some parts of Switzerland flattened pieces of metal in frog form are nailed onto doors to bring good luck to houses.

For those of us of an Anglo-Saxon persuasion, the prince of amphibians is Mr. Toad of Toad Hall, hero of the children's classic, The Wind in the Willows. Among our first visions of frogs was that of Mr. Toad at the wheel of his powerful motorcar, or disguised as an old woman and on the run from the police, or dressed in plus fours and Norfolk jacket, waving a sword as he reconquered Toad Hall from the Weasels and Stoats who had tried to rob him of his patrimony.

In 1733, Handel was confronted with a similar situation, when a rival opera company was established in London, sought and found royal patronage, and began to hire Handel's best singers away from him. Like Toad Hall, the London opera world was not big enough for two rulers, but Handel's victory, when the rival opera company closed up shop in 1737, was not so much a triumph as a stay of execution. Intelligent enough to know that opera seria had passed its sell-by date, Handel turned his musical genius to oratorio, taking his plots from Biblical sources and adding the majesty of the sound of choral singing, hoping that the combination would satisfy the quickly changing taste of music-mad London.

During the first three weeks of October 1738, Handel wrote them something to try: Israel in Egypt, an oratorio which recounts the story of Moses' success in leading his people from captivity in Egypt. He and his librettist Jennens took the text entirely from the Bible, something that was not to be done again until Messiah. In the First Part, the text recounts the mourning of the Sons of Israel, who much want to depart from Egypt, and Part Two recounts the plagues cast upon the Egyptians, among the first of which are the armies of frogs which covered the land.

The brief aria for alto, "Their land brought forth frogs," provides specific evidence of what the Lord chose to inflict upon the Egyptians: "Blotches and blains broke forth on man and beast," but it is the frogs who caught Handel's musical imagination. They do not stop at "the king's chambers" but spread and take over the entire aria. Dotted rhythm is a form of musical notation indicating that the note followed by the dot is to be prolonged, thus shortening the one after that. This creates a jerky, energetic rhythm much admired in the Baroque era. In this aria, the violins leap all over the place in dotted notation, starting with an octave and a fourth leap in the second bar, an even greater leap later on, and continuing to leap about even when the text has moved along to those "blotches and blains." Though the singing voice cannot match these leaps as beautifully as the violins, the singer does some virtuosic things and – quite fittingly – leaps up a fifth at the first mention of the word "frogs" itself. The musical tone is light, almost playful. Given the horrific plagues that are to follow, when Egypt will be wrapped in darkness and death, the musical image of these gamboling pests seems more playful than deadly.

ELEPHANT

ELEPHANT

With honour let desert be crowned
From: JUDAS MACCABAEUS
Act 3

Sweet flow the strains that strike my feasted ear;
angels might stoop from Heav'n to hear
the comely songs ye sing
to Israel's Lord and King.
But pause awhile: due obsequies prepare
to those who bravely fell in war.
To Eleazar special tribute pay –
through slaughtered troops he cut his way
to the distinguished elephant and, whelmed beneath
the stabbed monster, triumphed in a glorious death.

With honour let desert be crowned
the trumpet ne'er in vain shall sound;
but, all attentive to alarms,
the willing nations fly to arms
and, conquering or conquered, claim the prize
of happy earth or far more happy skies.

The elephant seems, perhaps, an odd vehicle for an example of proper sexual behavior, but this the elephant proved to be for the writers of medieval bestiaries, for elephant couples, man and wife, have sex only once, after which the female conceives immediately then sets in to wait two years for the birth. Anyone apt to think this a bitter blow against sexual freedom should contemplate the fate of the beaver, constrained, because of the medicinal value of his testicles, to gnaw them off and fling them at the feet of pursuing hunters. If he is again pursued by another hunter, all he had to do was hurl himself onto his back and open his legs to show that the problem had already been attended to. This explains his Latin name – Castor – for castration. (The hunter, obviously, is Satan, and the beaver sets the example – albeit a strong one – of what the virtuous man must do in order to control his natural tendency towards vices, sexual desire being high on the list.)

The elephant's name comes from the Greek, "eliphios," or mountain, for no larger animals were known to the compilers of the bestiaries. The paintings of the elephants in Medieval manuscripts, however, make one wonder just how well-known they actually were: some look like large, tusked wolves with lion paws(the artists found it difficult to conceive of an animal without hairy paws, and then there were those unbelievable ears) while others look like tusked pigs. In 1255, the King of France gave a live elephant to the King of England, and it is from that date that the animals pictured in English manuscripts, like one held at the St. Alban's Abbey, are recognizable as elephants. Before that, visual representations of elephants were as fabulous as those of the manticore or the basilisk.

Just as uncertain are the things known about them. For example, the elephant, as pictured in many of the manuscripts and as discussed in the literature, appears to have been the only kneeless quadruped. This accounts for the difficulty an elephant experiences when it falls down. Even the assistance of twelve adult elephants cannot get him to his feet; only by the arrival of a small, Insignificant Elephant can this be achieved, though the manuscripts remain vague about the details of the hydraulics involved here. The elephant's missing knees also created a certain difficulty in sleeping, which she could manage only by leaning against a tree. Thus all the wily hunter had to do was saw halfway through the tree against which an elephant chose to sleep, whereupon the elephant's weight would knock it over and she would crash to the ground along with the tree, thus presenting a helpless – because kneeless - prey to the hunter.

Over the course of centuries, many things had come to be known about the elephant. Pliny the Elder assured his readers that they live from two to three hundred years and hate mice, and Cassiodorus was convinced that the scent of its breath would cure headache. In battle with a unicorn, it is the elephant's stomach which is vulnerable to attack. The tanks of their day, elephants were vital in warfare; Aelian reported in the second century AD that the king of the Indians was preceded into battle by a hundred thousand elephants. After the defeat of Carthage, Roman weapons inspectors went though conquered territories hamstringing any elephant that exceeded the allotted number chained in the armories of their conquered enemies.

The Indians called him "barrus," and the noise that comes from his mouth is "barritus," from whence "baritone" for a deep voice. The recitative and aria from Handel's Judas Maccabaeus, however, is scored for the lighter tenor voice, the weight and heft of the aria being provided by the trumpet obbligato, evidence that "the trumpet ne'er in vain shall sound." Judas Maccabaeus sings the praises of Eleazar, who gave his life in return for victory in battle against Israel's enemies. Like the unicorn, he struck the hostile elephant from beneath, and like countless dragons, he died under the weight of the fallen beast, but "triumph'd in a glorious death."

MOTH

MOTH

Qual farfalletta giro a quel lume
From: PARTENOPE
Act 2, scene 7

Qual farfalletta
giro a quel lume
e il mio Cupido
le belle piume
ardendo va.

Quel brio m'alletta;
perché m'è fido,
la mia costanza
ogn' altra avanza,
cangiar non sa.

Like a butterfly
I flutter around the flame,
And my Cupid
Burns up his pretty wings
In the flame.

That young man draws me
With his fidelity,
I will be faithful to him.
No other temptation
Will change my heart.

The origin of the word "butterfly" is rich in legend: the name was given to the fly who came by night into dairies and drank itself to death in any uncovered vessel that held the cream that was to be churned into butter the following day. Strangely enough, however, the ancients and the writers of Bestiaries had precious little to say about the moth. They did realize that it came from the worm, as did many other unpleasant and destructive creatures, and they did manage to leave a pictorial record, though their drawings and paintings are not rich in detail and add little to the minimal written record.

To spend any time studying the paintings and drawings of animals as they are presented in medieval bestiaries is to realize and appreciate their simplicity: to turn from them to the pictorial record left by artists who painted little more than a century later is to come away marveling. The animals on the manuscript pages often remain curiously lifeless and formulaic, as though some of the artists (though 'illustrator' is perhaps a more accurate description) had been told about the animal or had heard it described, and thus the resulting portrait could as often mislead as represent. But let a century pass, and many of the paintings – one has but to glance at the work of an artist like Pisanello – show what can come of the combination of genius and direct observation.

The Angelo Mai Library in the northern Italian town of Bergamo has in its collection the sketchbook of Giovannino de` Grassi, the fourteenth-century painter and sculptor, which contains twenty-four sketches for a fantastic alphabet and seventy-seven other drawings, among them many animals and birds. One page – and bear in mind that this was only the artist's sketchbook – depicts three birds, painted with an accuracy and precision that a photographer would envy. There is also a beautifully detailed peacock in full display, and a pair of reclining deer, all of the same high quality.

Il Castello del Buonconsiglio in Trento has – from the fourteenth century, as well – a fresco cycle of the months, paintings that teem with plants and animals painted with great artistry. It is unnecessary to belabor the point: the artists of this period knew how to paint animals. The difference in quality between their work and that of the monks who illustrated the Bestiaries might lie in the fact that the monks were less likely to be motivated by artistic passion. The men who decorated the Bestiary manuscripts were men of the Middle Ages who followed tradition. God's design, they believed, had been handed down to them, and so they would follow the ancients in their thinking and in their illustrations. There is also to consider the fact that the descriptions presented to them often came from Crusaders who had gone to the East and had brought back the memory of the twisted images seen on ceramic and ruins left from pre-Islamic cultures. The pictorial images of heraldry, as well, presented only the sketchy profiles of beasts.

Galileo himself was later to advise that men not begin with the authority of Scriptural places, but "with real experiments and necessary demonstrations." Artists, real artists, thus opened their eyes to have a look about them at the way things were, not at the way they were told by the authorities that they were, or how they were reported to be by other men who had seen pictures or carvings of them.

Handel's Partenope, Queen of Naples, also opens her eyes and takes a look around her and sees, not God's creation, but four eligible young princes. Well, since one of them is really a woman disguised as a man, perhaps there are only three authentic candidates. Partenope nevertheless teases her way through the opera, flirting with this prince and that one, while in the background other characters do a bit of flirting themselves.

In the second act, finally forced to make up her mind about which prince to choose, Partenope decides to accept the offer of Armindo, the prince of Rhodes. By way of explanation, she likens her love-struck condition to that of the moth, who flutters around "the fatal light" of the candle. In the music one hears the fluttering of the wings of the moth as it draws ever closer to the dangerous flames of love. Though Partenope does not have a very good track record in constancy, she insists that she will prove "constant in my turn," but what the listener hears in the down up, down up rhythm of her aria is the fluttering of the wings of the moth as it flirts with the temptation offered by the candle's flame. She too, circles repeatedly around the flame of this young prince, an obsession repeated in her music: the vocal and violin parts are identical in several bars, a rarity in Handel's writing. Obsession is, after all, an inability to change things: thus, like the moth that flutters in the same pattern, Partenope is unable to break free her own obsession with the flame of love.

STAG

STAG

Cervo altier
From: OTTONE, RE DI GERMANIA
Act 1, scene 5

Cervo altier, poichè prostrò
combattendo un gran rival,
corre lieto alla cervetta.

E la pugna sua felice
forse ancora a lei ridice
che, da lungi, il rimirò
e sollecita l'aspetta.

The noble stag
Defeats his rival
And returns to his beloved.

And his happy combat
Perhaps he recounts again to her
Who from afar, had watched him
And now anxiously awaits him.

The majesty of the stag has slipped into our culture from all manner of places. Pliny the Elder, Lucretius, Lucan, Isidore of Seville – the usual suspects – all praise the stag and his mate, the doe: much of what they say would eventually be used by Christian writers for their own purposes, for they found in the behavior attributed to the stag many qualities which could be used as examples of good Christian deportment.

Not only Christians valued the animal: among the Anglo-Saxon treasure found at Sutton Hoo is a scepter from the Seventh Century bearing the image of a stag. Modern mythology, too, has as one of its most prominent symbols a stag, for is it not this which Bambi will become? Surely an entire generation has had burned into its visual memory the death of Bambi's mother as well as the great explosion of testosterone that is Bambi's great battle. Indeed, "Bambi" has become as much a metonym as "White House" or "Pampers." (There is a restaurant in Innsbruck which once listed "Bambi" on the menu.)

As early as the first century before Christ, writers disputed the qualities of the stag. While Pliny the Elder was certain that stags could serve as a kind of vacuum cleaner and pull snakes out of their holes with their breath to destroy them, Lucretius pooh-poohed the idea. Regardless of his denial, the belief in a natural antipathy between stags and snakes, as well as a favorable view of the general utility of stags, percolated into Western culture. This can be seen in Lucan's belief that snakes will be killed by the smell of a burning stag antler and Pliny's firm conviction that the smell will also prevent an attack of epilepsy. When feeling themselves ill or old, stags eat snakes and, somehow resistant to the poison, thus find themselves renewed to health and vigor. Further, since they are animals which are never feverish, an ointment made of their marrow will "settle heats in sick men."

Stags could not only restore themselves but also humans, as they did the soul and life of the man who became the man known as Saint Eustace but whose career towards sanctity began when he was a Roman general named Placidus. Out hunting one day, he chased a stag who turned to face the man hunting him, only to reveal an image of Jesus between his antlers. That was enough to convince Placidus – who became Eustace – of the validity and superiority of the new god. No sooner were he and his family baptized, however, than bad fortune began to stalk him. He quickly lost wealth, servants, and family and became a sort of Christian Job. He did not, however, lose his faith, whereupon everything was soon returned to him. Until, that is, he refused to sacrifice to the pagan gods, which caused the Emperor Trajan to have the whole lot of them stuffed into the bronze statue of an ox, where they were roasted to death. He is thus the patron saint of huntsmen, and of anyone suffering adversity, but not of bakers.

Many of the illustrations in the Medieval bestiaries show antlered stags swimming in a line, often with their heads upon the rump of the one in front, as they try to cross a river or lake. There is an early Thirteenth Century manuscript in the Fitzwilliam Library in Cambridge which shows four of them in a row crossing a body of water and another, almost contemporaneous, in the Bibliotheque Nationale de France, showing the same scene. This was one of the ideas that appealed to Christian writers, for it served as an example of the way in which Christians, passing through the stream of life, should aid those who weaken or tire.

The stag appears in an aria for Ottone, the hero of Handel's opera of the same name. His simile aria makes reference to something from the real world of stags: their tendency to fight to the death over possession of the female. In his simile aria, "Cervo altier," Ottone sees himself as a stag battling "un gran rival" for the attentions of "la cervetta." He will, of course, be victorious in this, as is demonstrated in the vigorous, confident leaps of his coloratura.

PHOENIX

PHOENIX

Io son qual fenice
From: ADMETO, RE DI TESSAGLIA
Act 2, scene 1

116

Io son qual fenice
risorta dal foco
e in me a poco a poco
risorge l'amor.

Il cor già mi dice
ch'il caro mio bene,
godendo, a me viene
e scaccia il dolor.

Like the phoenix,
Reborn from the flames,
In me, slowly, slowly,
Love is reborn.

My heart tells me
That my beloved
Is coming happily to me
And will cast away my pain.

The medieval bestiaries are rather short on information about worms, which is strange, given the filth which abounded in homes, cities, even castles. They depict creatures which could easily be mistaken for striped fish, and the accounts given of their nature and activity do little more than list the places where worms are found or from which they originate: meat, earth, air, flesh, wood, clothes, or leaves. Though their precise place of origin might be vague, it was believed that they sprang to life without the aid of intercourse and that they moved by stretching and constricting their bodies. Many creatures were included in the category of worms: scorpions, leeches, millipedes, ticks, and all manner of unpleasant crawly things.

How puzzling this is: surely the worm in its various manifestations was a creature which the readers and writers of bestiaries – indeed, anyone with eyes – would have seen often and everywhere, and yet little effort is made to tell stories about their origin or to make moral links between their behavior and that of humans.

There was, however, one creature that sprang, at least in some versions, from a worm. It is the Arabian Phoenix, that most wondrous of birds: magnificent in purple and gold and capable of eternal - however interrupted - life. This bird, as written about by Herodotus, Ovid, Lucan, and Pliny, lives five hundred or more years, and when he senses that he is soon to die, he repairs himself to a tree, wherein he builds a nest. In this nest, he dies, and some time after his death, a worm is discovered, from which a new phoenix will rise.

During the centuries that elapsed between the accounts of the pagan writers and that of the Seventh Century writer, Isidore of Seville, the Phoenix became both a suicide and a pyromaniac, for the legend took on what has become its best-known element: the Phoenix, nearing the end of its life, builds a nest of rich spices and immolates itself by turning to face the sun and flapping its wings to create a fire, only to spring back to life from its own ashes after three days.

This image of purified rebirth was irresistible for Christian writers. St. Ambrose, writing his brother's funeral oration in 375, gave the Phoenix myth as evidence for human resurrection: "There is a bird in Arabia called the phoenix. After it dies, it comes back to life, restored by the renovating fluid in its own flesh. Shall we believe that men alone are not restored to life again?" His contemporary, Lactantius, is equally certain about the spiritual nature of resurrection, though he is uncertain about the bird's sex: "whether male or female or neither. . . ." The symbolism is perfect: just as Christ is sacrificed and is reborn, so too the consenting Christian, though his body perishes, will be purified and reborn in Christ.

What might be called the Elephant Problem is evident in the way the artists of Medieval bestiaries presented the Phoenix. Now, it is safe to presume that, though most had not, some Europeans at least had seen elephants, either in Africa or India, and had brought back sketches or descriptions. But they had seen them. The fact that no one – at least to the best of my knowledge – had actually seen a phoenix in no way prevented the artists from painting them.

One bird presented in a 12th century British manuscript is indeed identifiably a bird, though the bird it most resembles is, unfortunately, a dodo. The Fitzwilliam Museum has a manuscript with another bird, this one with party-colored stripes and looking more wall-papered than feathered. Manuscript phoenixes are occasionally rash in their choice of location for immolation. Those who select flat surfaces, with fires burning beneath, run the risk of looking suspiciously like, well, like a summer barbecue. Those who choose to insert themselves for burning within concave nests fare far better, at least in the visual sense.

However unlikely it might be that Handel had much first-hand experience of the phoenix, the aria he wrote for the soprano in Admeto accurately conveys the joy that comes when hope causes love to rise from its own ashes. The aria was written for one of his most famous singers, Faustina Bordoni Hasse, and was sung in a benefit concert of the opera. Curiously enough, this is one of the few arias known to have been sung by both of those arch-rivals, Faustina and Cuzzoni, though

Faustina sang it when she played Alceste and Cuzzoni when she sang Antigona.

The triadic coloratura gives a sense of someone doing handsprings for joy, for her heart tells her that her beloved is on his way back to her, and she is sure that his return will drive away all suffering. These handsprings, however, are a bit premature, for she has yet to discover that, during the time she has been agreeing to die in his place, the man she loves has been taking up with another woman.

TURTLE DOVE

TURTLE DOVE

Fuor di periglio
From: FLORIDANTE
Act 2, scene 6

ROSSANE:
Ormai tutta silenzio è l'alta notte.
Tu solo, fida e armata scorta,
vanne con Floridante,
ove l'aspetta Elmira;
me trovarete pronta a quel secreto
varco dove comprata
della vil guardia è già per noi la fede.

TIMANTE:
Vado, pietoso Amore,
conduci a secondar fuga sì ardita
il silenzio ed il sonno in nostra aita.

ROSSANE & TIMANTE:
Fuor di periglio
di fiero artiglio,
colombe amate
saremo allor.

Accompagnate
da un sol consiglio,
innamorate
da un sol ardor.

ROSSANE:

> At last the deep night is all silence.
> Go alone, faithful and armed guide,
> with Floridante where Elmira expects him.
> You shall find me ready at the secret
> Passage, where the fidelity
> Of the vile guards has been bought for us.

TIMANTE:

> I go. Let compassionate Love
> Bring fortune to so bold a flight,
> With silence and sleep to our aid.

ROSSANE & TIMANTE:

> Out of danger
> Of a fierce talon,
> We shall then be
> Amorous doves.
>
> Accompanied by a single council,
> Enamoured
> By a single ardour.

"A wonderful bird is the pelican
Whose beak can hold more than its belly can."

This doggerel rhyme remains from my childhood and continues, after more than half a century, to delight me. It joked with language while pointing to one of the marvels of what I only much later learned was called ornithology, for the beak of a pelican does indeed appear to hold far more than its belly can.

Language also enters into a discussion of the turtle dove, for the name is onomatopoeic, "turtur," being an orthographic attempt to capture the sound of its call. The turtle dove is a shy and retiring bird which lives in solitude in the desert and on the tops of mountains. After moulting, she hides in the holes in trees. When she has young, she will fill her nest with squill leaves, knowing that wolves, who do not like the smell of these leaves, will be repelled by them. (Apparently expert at smells, the turtle dove has apparently failed to observe that wolves are not expert at climbing trees.)

Pliny, discussing in his Natural History the habits of the turtle dove's nearest relatives, the pigeons, observes that none will violate the laws of marital fidelity. At times, alas, the male might act in an imperious manner, but the female will, of course, put up with it. (Of course.) However much the males might entertain suspicions of the female's fidelity, Pliny puts these doubts quickly to rest with his assurance that the female is, by nature, incapable of such a thing. It might here be observed, that this is the same Pliny who, when he was the commander of the Roman fleet in Southern Italy, both failed to consider the seriousness of the volcanic eruption taking place around him and asked to be put ashore the better to observe it, thus becoming the most famous victim of the eruption of Vesuvius in 79 AD, the eruption that buried Pompeii and Herculaneum.

The timidity and natural virtue of the turtle dove destined her to become the poster bird of virtue, into which role she was impressed by the writers of Bestiaries — as well as many others - and turned into a symbol of marital fidelity. Geoffrey Chaucer, in The Parliament of Fowles (c.1381) uses the turtledove as the spokesbird of the seed eaters, who declares that, " . . . if my lady died, I would have no other mate . . . I would be hers until death take me."

Chaucer was in step with the writers of his time, who consigned the turtledove to long lives of widowed chastity. At least he so consigned the female turtle dove, as did many of the writers of Bestiaries, who enjoined women to take to their hearts the high esteem in which even birds held the state of widowhood. So great is the betrayal of the experience of love by the death of her husband - women were reminded by these texts - that she comes to hate the idea of marriage and the marriage bed: the grief of loss far exceeds the delights of love.

Guillaume le Clerc, a Thirteenth Century French cleric, while still insisting that women will want to remain faithful to memory after death has taken their husbands, has seen a thing or two of life outside the monastery and thus realizes that a man, "before he has eaten two meals desires to have another woman in his arms."

The duet "Fuor di periglio" from Floridante was given by Handel to the secondary lovers, Rossane and Timante, and they use it to give the lie to Guillaume. Once out of peril, they sing, they will bill and coo as do the turtle doves, united by a single passion. The text encouraged Handel to write one of his most charming and single-minded duets. The unity of their love is mirrored in Handel's having written the duet for two similar treble voices, often united in parallel thirds, separated by only the harmonious interval of a third. The accompanying pairs of instruments – the familiar pairs of oboes and violins and the less familiar pairs of horns and bassoons – give more evidence of unity. The billing and cooing of the singers is echoed - at least in the register where Handel chooses to put them – in the horns and bassoons.

Love in opera seldom flows smoothly, but in this duet Handel suggests what is possible when it does. There are no surprises, no contrasting themes, and no change is offered by the middle section. The smooth flow of the music serves to reflect the united purpose of the two lovers, as does Handel's use of the Baroque technique of "chain of suspensions," heard when one voice moves to dissonance, only to be joined by its partner, which immediately resolves the dissonance into consonance. In this way, Handel illustrates the text while still maintaining the smooth flow of the piece.

Sources

LION
Qual leon che fere irato
From: ARIANNA IN CRETA, 1733, HWV 32
Dramma
Libretto: unknown (after Pietro Pariati)
Aria of Tauride, act 2, scene 6

SNAKE
L'angue o eso mai riposa
From: GIULIO CESARE IN EGITTO, 1723, HWV 17
Dramma
Libretto: Nicola Haym (after Giacomo Francesco Bussani)
Recitative and aria of Sesto, act 2, scene 6

NIGHTINGALE
Nasconde l'usignol' in alti rami il nido
From: DEIDAMIA, 1740, HWV 42
Melodramma
Libretto: Paolo Rolli
Recitative and aria of Deidamia, act 1, scene 5

BEE
Vedi l'ape
From: BERENICE, REGINA D EGITTO, 1736/37, HWV 38
Dramma
Libretto: unknown (after Antonio Salvi)
Aria of Fabio, act 1, scene 3

135

SILVER DOVE

O that I on wings could rise
From: THEODORA, 1749, HWV 68
Oratorio
Libretto: Thomas Morell
Recitative and aria of Theodora, act 2, scene 2

TIGER

Sta nell'Ircana pietrosa tana
From: ALCINA, 1735, HWV 34
Dramma
Libretto: unknown
Aria of Ruggiero, act 3, scene 3

FROGS

Their land brought forth frogs
From: ISRAEL IN EGYPT, 1738, HWV 54
Oratorio
Libretto: probably Charles Jennens (after Book of Exodus and Psalms)
Air (alto), Part II

ELEPHANT

With honour let desert be crowned
From: JUDAS MACCABAEUS, 1746, HWV 63
Oratorio
Libretto: Thomas Morell (after 1 Maccabees and Flavius Josephus)
Recitative and Aria of Judas Maccabaeus, act 3

MOTH

Qual farfalletta giro a quel lume
From: PARTENOPE, 1730, HWV 27
Dramma
Libretto: unknown (after Silvio Stampiglia)
Aria of Partenope, act 2, scene 7

STAG

Cervo altier
From: OTTONE, RE DI GERMANIA, 1722, HWV 15
Dramma
Libretto: Nicola Francesco Haym
  (after Stefano Benedetto Pallavicino)
Aria of Ottone, act 1, scene 5

PHOENIX

Io son qual fenice
From: ADMETO, RE DI TESSAGLIA, 1726, HWV 22
Dramma
Libretto: unknown (after Aurelio Aureli / Ortensio Mauro)
Aria of Antigona, act 2, scene 1

TURTLE DOVE

Fuor di periglio
From: FLORIDANTE, 1721, HWV 14
Dramma
Libretto: Paolo Rolli (after Francesco Silvani)
Recitative and duet of Timante and Rossane, act 2, scene 6

Quoted from the edition of the German Händel Society:
Georg Friedrich Händel: Complete Works, Leipzig 1858 – 1902

Il Complesso Barocco: Cast

Soprano
Karina Gauvin (nightingale, silver dove, moth, phoenix, turtle dove)

Mezzo-soprano
Ann Hallenberg (lion, snake, tiger, frogs, stag, turtle dove)

Tenors
Paul Agnew (elephant)
Anicio Zorzi Giustiniani (bee)

First Violins
Dmitry Sinkovsky
Alfia Bakieva
Daniela Nuzzoli
Laura Corolla

Second Violins
Boris Begelman
Isabella Bison
Yayoi Masuda

Violas
Giulio D'Alessio
Elisa Imbalzano

Cellos
Catherine Jones
Ludovico Minasi

Double bass
Riccardo Coelati Rama

Oboes
Yann Miriel
Taka Kitazato

Bassoons
Andrea Bressan
Michele Fattori

Horns
Dileno Baldin
Francesco Meucci

Trumpet
Hannes Rux

Archlute
Pier Luigi Ciapparelli

Harpsichord
Andrea Perugi
Alan Curtis

Recording producer: Laurence Heym
Recording: Villa San Fermo, Lonigo, April 2010
Produced by Giulio D'Alessio

All of the recordings on the enclosed CD were made specifically for this project by *Il Complesso Barocco* under the baton of Alan Curtis, with the exception of *Vedi l'ape,* which was taken from BERENICE, REGINA D'EGITTO, also recorded by Alan Curtis and *Il Complesso Barocco* (June 2010, EMI, Virgin Classics).

DONNA LEON was born in New Jersey in 1942. Venice has been home to her since 1981. Commissario Guido Brunetti has brought Leon international fame, but there is another hero in her life: George Frideric Handel. Donna Leon travels far and wide to attend performances of Handel's music and she is a patron of productions of his operas with the Il Complesso Barocco ensemble under the baton of Alan Curtis.

ALAN CURTIS was born in Mason, Michigan, in 1934. In 1979 he founded Il Complesso Barocco, an international ensemble dedicated to Baroque music on original instruments and particularly to the operas of George Frideric Handel. For their Handel-recordings they were awarded the German Record Critics' Award in 2003 as well as the International Handel Recording Prize on several occasions.

MICHAEL SOWA was born in Berlin in 1945. From 1965 to 1972 he studied at the Berlin School of Fine Arts. His illustrations have appeared in publications such as *Titanic, Die Zeit,* and *The New Yorker* in addition to a great many books. In 1995 he received the Olaf Gulbransson Prize, and in 2004 he was awarded the Berlin Book Prize in the children's book category.